Published by Al-Kawthar Publishing

Copyright © Al-Kawthar Publishing 2021

All rights reserved. This publication is protected by copyright owned by Al-Kawthar Publishing and you may not reproduce, disseminate, or communicate to the public the whole or a substantial amount part thereof except as permitted at law or with the prior written consent of Al-Kawthar Publishing.

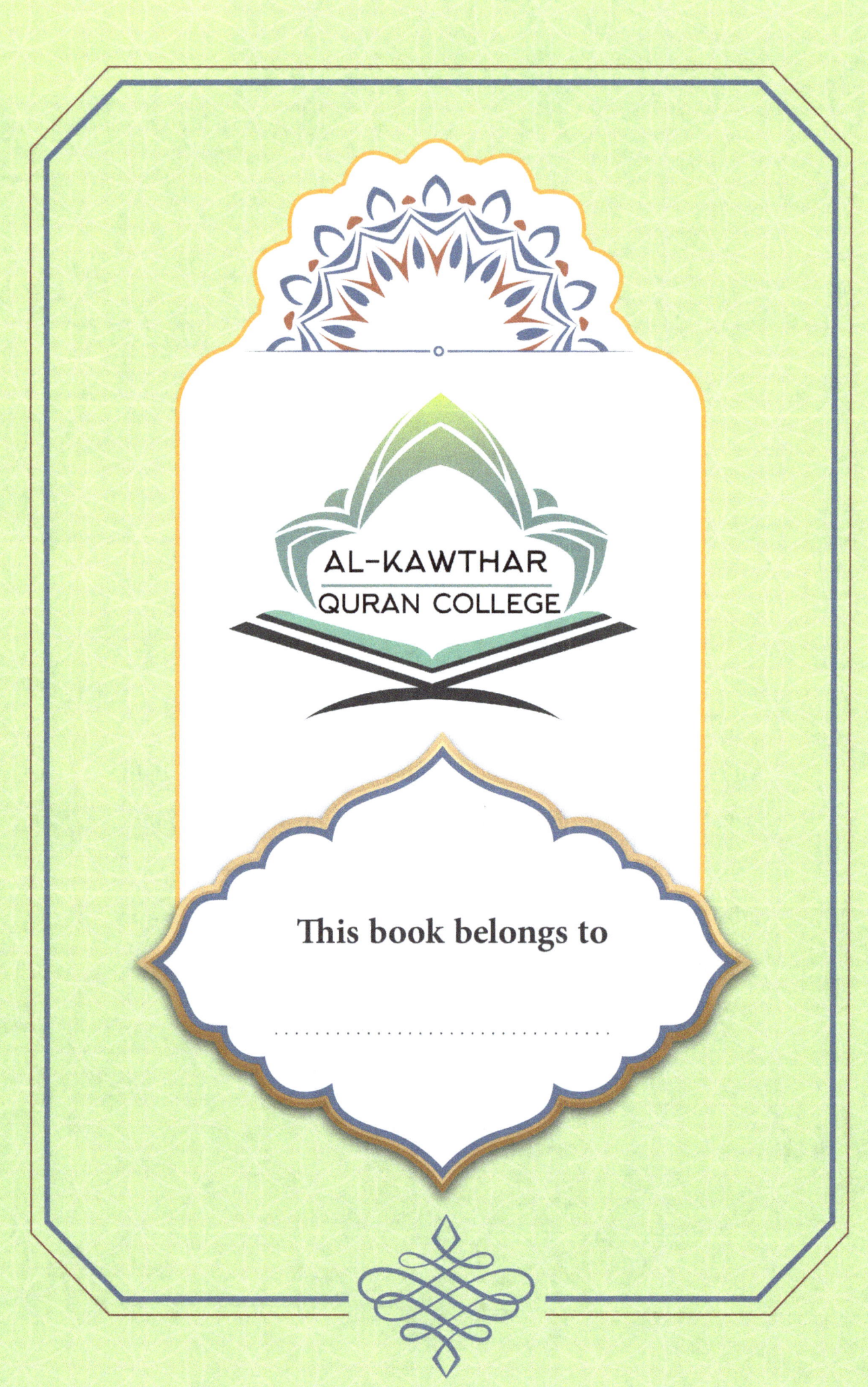

بسم الله الرحمن الرحيم

About the author

Sheikh Mohammad Dehnavi completed the memorisation of the entire Holy Quran in the city of Isfahan in 2002 at the age of 11. He commenced his Hawza studies at the age of 18, by joining the Shahidayn seminary in Qum. He completed the 10th level of Hawza in 2019. He has started his Bahthul Khaarij studies (highest level of Islamic education) via online correspondence from Sydney.

Sheikh Mohammad has extensive experience in the field of Quranic, Arabic and Islamic teaching in various countries.

He has written two books in the field of Quranic sciences:

'The Topical Memorisation': written in Arabic, this book is a guide to memorising the Holy Quran based on topics. Published in 2015 Qum

'Popular Everyday Sayings rooted in the Holy Quran': written in Farsi, published in 2009, Qum.

Currently, he is based in Sydney Australia where he has been teaching memorization of the holy Quran and Tajweed at different Islamic centres and schools. At this stage he is working on the project of writing curriculums on different aspects of the holy Quran such as reading proficiency, Tajweed, comprehension and memorization for the English-speaking students.

Table of Contents

Goals — page 6

Syllabus — page 7

Surah Memorisation plan — page 8

Learning plan — page 9

Instructions for the teachers — page 11

Lesson 1 — page 12

Letters with Kasrah

Lesson 2 — page 23

Letters with Kasrah

Lesson 3 — page 34

Letters with Dammah

Lesson 4 — page 45

Letters with Dammah

Lesson 5 — page 57

Fatha, Kasrah and Dammah

Lesson 6 — page 67

Fatha, Kasrah and Dammah

Lesson 7 — page 77

Fatha, Kasrah and Dammah

Lesson 8 — page 86

Fatha, Kasrah and Dammah

Lesson 9 — page 95

Revision

Goals

By the end of this book, students will:

- Be able to recognise, pronounce and write the letters with Fatha, Kasrah and Dammah
- Be able to read grouped letters and simple words with Fatha, Kasrah and Dammah
- Have memorised and understood the concept of Surah Al-Qadr and Al-Fil
- Have learned the meaning of the Quranic words of Surah Al-Qadr and Al-Fil
- Have memorized two Quranic moral sentences and their concepts

Syllabus

Week	Lesson	Surah	Revision	Meaning of Quranic words	Quran by topic
1	Letters with Kasrah	Al-Qadr	Al-Sharh Al-Kafirun		Revision و بالوالدين إحسانا
2	Letters with Kasrah	Al-Qadr	Al-Qadr	ليلة القدر، خير ، شهر	Revision و بالوالدين إحسانا
3	Letters with Dammah	Al-Qadr	Al-Qadr	الـملائكة ، سلام	Revision و بالوالدين إحسانا
4	Letters with Dammah	Al-Qadr	Al-Qadr	Revision ليلة القدر، خير ، شهر الملائكة ، سلام	ربّ زدني علما
5	Fatha, Kasrah and Dammah	Al-Fil	Al-Fil Al-Qadr		Revision ربّ زدني علما
6	Fatha, Kasrah and Dammah	Al-Fil	Al-Fil Al-Qadr	الفيل ، كيد	Revision ربّ زدني علما
7	Fatha, Kasrah and Dammah	Al-Fil	Al-Fil Al-Qadr	طير ، حجارة	Revision ربّ زدني علما
8	Fatha, Kasrah and Dammah	Al-Fil	Al-Fil Al-Qadr	Revision الفيل ، كيد طير ، حجارة	فأصلحوا بين أخويكم
9	Revision	Revision Al-Fil Al-Qadr		Revision on previous words	Revision ربّ زدني علما فأصلحوا بين أخويكم
10	Assessment				

Surah Memorisation plan

Level	Book	Surah
Preliminary Level	Book 1	Al-Ikhlas & Al-Asr
	Book 2	Al-Nas & Al-Falaq
	Book 3	Al-Fatiha & Al-Kawthar
	Book 4	Al-Nasr & Quraysh
Level 1	Book 1	Al-Masad & Al-Takathur
	Book 2	Al-Qariah & Al-Maun
	Book 3	Al-Kafirun & Al-Sharh
	Book 4	Al-Qadr & Al-Fil
Level 2	Book 1	Al-Shams & Al-Tin
	Book 2	Al-Homazah & Al-Adiyat
	Book 3	Al-Duha & Al-Zalzalah
	Book 4	Al-Layl
Level 3	Book 1	Al-Ghashiyah
	Book 2	Al-Alaq & Al-Ala
	Book 3	Al-Bayyinah & Al-Balad
	Book 4	Al-Infitar & Al-Tariq
Level 4	Book 1	Al-Fajr
	Book 2	Al-Burooj
	Book 3	Al-Inshiqaq
	Book 4	Al-Takwir

Learning plan

Preliminary Level

By the end of this level students will:

- Be able to recognise, pronounce and write the letters with fatha in their main form
- Have memorised and understood the concept of 7 short Suwar of Juz 30 and Surah Al-Fatihah
- Have learned the meaning of the Quranic words of the memorised Suwar
- Have memorised 8 Quranic moral sentences and their concepts

Level 1

By the end of this level students will:

- Be able to recognise, pronounce and write the letters (in single and joined form) with fatha, kasrah and dammah (Short Vowels)
- Be able to read simple words/ short sentences with fatha, kasrah and dammah
- Have memorised and understood the concept of 8 short Suwar of Juz 30
- Have learned the meaning of the Quranic words of the memorised Suwar
- Have memorised 8 Quranic moral sentences and their concepts

Level 2

By the end of this level students will:

- Be able to recognise, pronounce and write the letters with Sukoon, Long Vowels, Shaddah and Tanween
- Be able to read long sentences from the Quran
- Have memorised and understood the concept of 7 Suwar of Juz 30
- Have learned the meaning of the Quranic words of the memorised Suwar
- Have memorised 8 Quranic moral sentences and their concepts

Level 3

By the end of this level students will:

- Have studied the rules of silent letters (Hamzat Al-Wasl, Lam Shamsiyah, etc), stopping rules
- Be able to read verses from the Quran
- Have memorised and understood the concept of 7 Suwar of Juz 30
- Have learned the meaning of the Quranic words of the memorised Suwar
- Have memorised 8 Quranic moral sentences and their concepts

Level 4

By the end of this level students will:

- Have studied the Tajweed rules and are able to apply it in their Quran recitation
- Have memorised and understood the concept of some long Suwar of Juz 30
- Have learned the meaning of the Quranic words of the memorised Suwar
- Have memorised 8 Quranic moral sentences and their concepts

Learning Roadmap

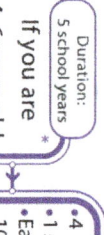

If you are 4-6 years old
Duration: 5 school years *

→ **Preliminary Level**
- 4 books
- 1 school year (40 weeks)
- Each book covers 10 weeks (three 45min sessions per week)

If you are 6-8 years old
Duration: 4 school years

→ **Level 1**
- 4 books
- 1 school year (40 weeks)
- Each book covers 10 weeks (three 45min sessions per week)

↓ **Level 2**
- 4 books
- 1 school year (40 weeks)
- Each book covers 10 weeks (three 45min sessions per week)

↓ **Level 3**
- 4 books
- 1 school year (40 weeks)
- Each book covers 10 weeks (three 45min sessions per week)

↓ **Level 4**
- 4 books
- 1 school year (40 weeks)
- Each book covers 10 weeks (three 45min sessions per week)

If you are 8-10 years old
Duration: 3 school years

→ **Concise version of Level 1**
- 2 books
- 20 weeks
- Each book covers 10 weeks (three 45min sessions per week)

↓ **Concise version of Level 2**
- 2 books
- 20 weeks
- Each book covers 10 weeks (three 45min sessions per week)

↓ **Level 3**
- 4 books
- 1 school year (40 weeks)
- Each book covers 10 weeks (three 45min sessions per week)

↓ **Level 4**
- 4 books
- 1 school year (40 weeks)
- Each book covers 10 weeks (three 45min sessions per week)

If you are 10-16 years old
Duration: 2 school years

→ **Concise version of Level 1**
- 1 book
- 10 weeks
- Each book covers 10 weeks (three 45min sessions per week)

↓ **Concise version of Level 2**
- 1 book
- 10 weeks
- Each book covers 10 weeks (three 45min sessions per week)

↓ **Concise version of Level 3**
- 2 books
- 20 weeks
- Each book covers 10 weeks (three 45min sessions per week)

↓ **Level 4**
- 4 books
- 1 school year (40 weeks)
- Each book covers 10 weeks (three 45min sessions per week)

→ **Quran Understanding** **

* This curriculum is suitable and recommended to be taught at junior school.
** Pre-requisite for entry into 3 years Quran Understanding course is completion of Level 4 of Quran Reading course.

Instructions for the teachers:

Al-Kawthar Quran College is honored to present you with series of educational books on teaching different aspects of the holy Quran in an integrated manner to students from English-speaking background.

Following points aim to provide brief instructions and explanation about the logic and methodology of the Quran teaching curriculum:

1. Each level is designed in 4 different books. Each book is covered over a 10 week term. There are 5 levels (20 books) covered over 5 years. By the end of the 5 year program, the students will be able to:
- recite the holy Quran proficiently with the application of the Tajweed rules.
- memorise different Suwar (chapters) of Juz' 30 with brief and simple comprehension.
- understand common and important Quranic vocabularies of the memorised Suwar.
- memorise Akhlaqi (moral) verses of the holy Quran and understand their concept.

2. Arabic alphabets are taught using myriad of activities and games.
3. Memorization of different chapters is done through practical Quranic games.
4. The Arabic alphabets should be taught using the sound they make and not their name (There will be a separate lesson for the abbreviated (almuqattaah) letters in the more advanced stages).
5. In teaching the Arabic letters do not use its English equivalent. Some Arabic letters do not have English equivalent such as ع.
6. Memorization of each Surah is designed to happen over 4 weeks (except chapter Al-Fatiha). The teacher should divide the teaching of each chapter over 3 weeks and dedicate the fourth week to revision.
7. Before teaching any new verse, revise the previous taught verses.
8. Try to encourage students to memorize the moral (Akhlaqi) verses with its meaning.
9. In order to teach the common Quranic vocabularies, the teacher should recite each word with its meaning and ask students to repeat after their recitation.
10. For any question, comments or suggestions please contact the author via the following email: Info@alkawtharcollege.com

Lesson 1
Kasrah

إِ بِ تِ ثِ
جِ حِ خِ دِ ذِ رِ زِ
سِ شِ صِ ضِ

Letter Section — Letter Recognition

Letter pronunciation and Writing

Listen and repeat the target letters with kasrah after your teacher

Letter Section
Letter pronunciation and Writing

Activity 1
Trace the letters with kasrah

Letter Section
Letter pronunciation and Writing

Activity 2 — Connect the letter with fatha with its matching letter with kasrah

Letter Section

Letter pronunciation and Writing

Activity 3 — Write the letters with kasrah

إِ ءِ إِ	بِ بِ	تِ تِ ةِ ةِ
ثِ ثِ	جِ جِ	حِ حِ
خِ خِ	دِ دِ	ذِ ذِ
رِ رِ	زِ زِ	سِ سِ
شِ شِ	صِ صِ	ضِ ضِ

Letter Section
Letter pronunciation and Writing

Activity 4 — Circle the letters with kasrah and write them in the box provided, then read the words

بَخِلَ	تَجِدَ	حَبِطَ	قَبِلَ
			بِ

أَثِمَ	يَبِسَ	رَحِمَ	شَجَرَةِ

Activity 5 — Read the words, then trace them

وَجِلَ	صَحِبَ	تَجِبَ
وَجِلَ	صَحِبَ	تَجِبَ

رَبِحَ	لَبِثَ	إِرَمَ
رَبِحَ	لَبِثَ	إِرَمَ

17

Letter Section
Letter pronunciation and Writing

Activity 6 — Read the words, then trace them and separate them in to letters

إِ ءِ إِ	بِ بِ	تِ تِ ةِ ةِ
إِبِلَ	لَبِثَ	شَجَرَةِ
إِبِلَ	لَبِثَ	شَجَرَةِ
إِ + بِ + لَ		

ثِ ثِ	جِ جِ	حِ حِ
أَثِمَ	تَجِدَ	صَحِبَ
أَثِمَ	تَجِدَ	صَحِبَ

خِ خِ	دِ	ذِ
بَخِلَ	رَدِفَ	أَذِنَ
بَخِلَ	رَدِفَ	أَذِنَ

18

Quran Section

(Memorising the Surah and understanding the concept)

بِسْمِ اللَّهِ الرَّحْمَنِ الرَّحِيمِ

إِنَّا أَنْزَلْنَاهُ فِي لَيْلَةِ الْقَدْرِ (1) وَمَا أَدْرَاكَ مَا لَيْلَةُ الْقَدْرِ (2)

لَيْلَةُ الْقَدْرِ خَيْرٌ مِنْ أَلْفِ شَهْرٍ (3)

تَنَزَّلُ الْمَلَائِكَةُ وَالرُّوحُ فِيهَا بِإِذْنِ رَبِّهِمْ مِنْ كُلِّ أَمْرٍ (4)

سَلَامٌ هِيَ حَتَّى مَطْلَعِ الْفَجْرِ (5)

Surah Al-Qadr

This Surah talks about the night of Qadr in the month of Ramadan. This night was the night that the Quran was sent down by Allah.

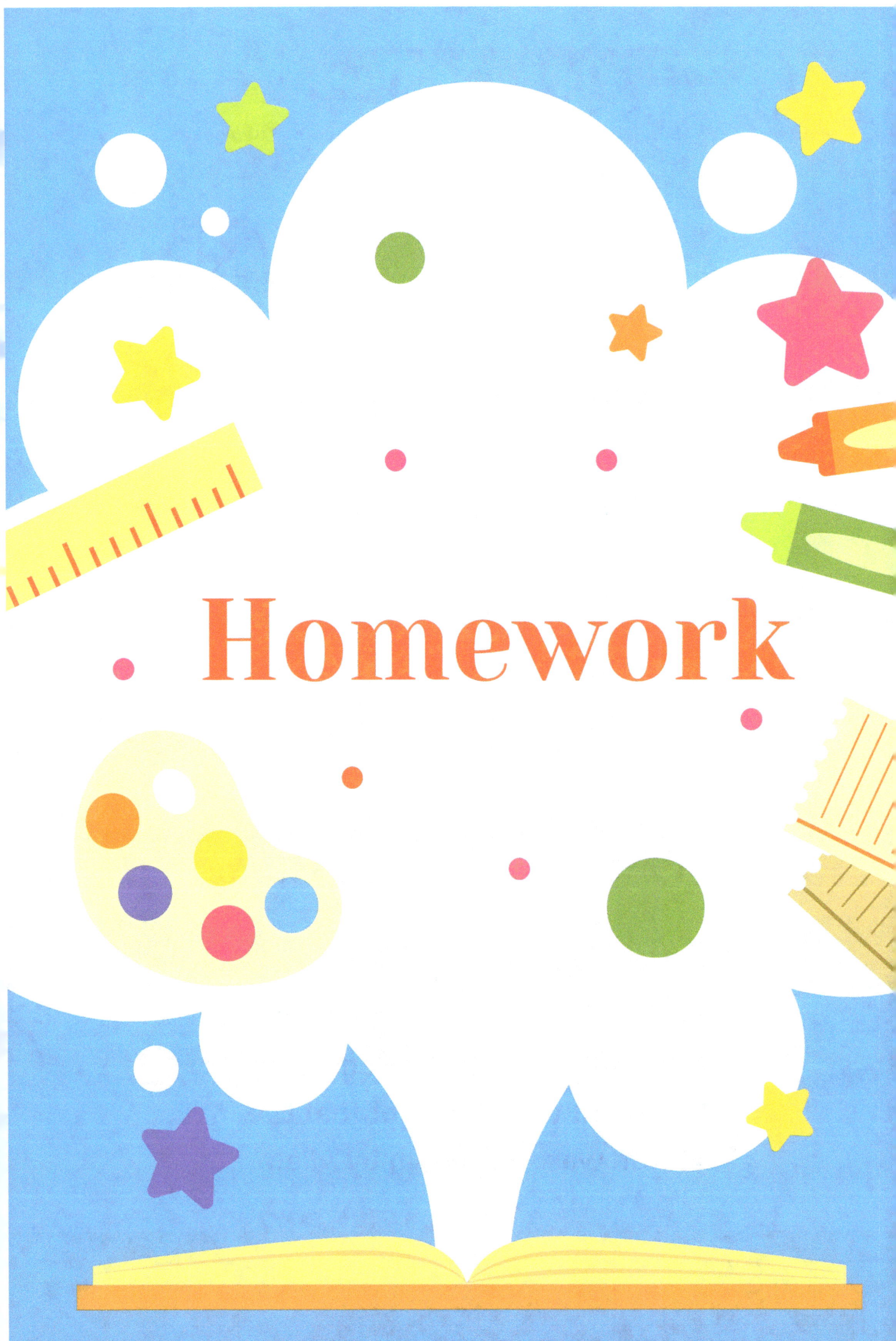

Homework

Activity 1 — Trace/write a kasrah where necessary

إِ إِ ءِ	بِ بِ	ةِ تِ تِ
ثِ ثِ	جِ جِ	حِ حِ
خِ خِ	دِ	ذِ
رِ	زِ	سِ سِ
شِ شِ	صِ صِ	ضِ ضِ

Homework

Activity 2 — Write the letters with kasrah

إِ ءِ إِ	بِ بِ	تِ تِ ةِ تِ ةِ

| ثِ ثِ | جِ جِ | حِ حِ |

| خِ خِ | دِ دِ | ذِ ذِ ذِ |

| رِ رِ | زِ زِ | سِ سِ |

| شِ شِ | صِ صِ | ضِ ضِ |

Lesson 2
Kasrah

طِ ظِ عِ غِ فِ قِ كِ لِ

مِ نِ هِ وِ يِ

Letter Section — Letter Recognition

Letter pronunciation and Writing

Listen and repeat the target letters with kasrah after your teacher

Letter Section
Letter pronunciation and Writing

Activity 1
Trace the letters with kasrah

Letter Section
Letter pronunciation and Writing

Activity 2 — Connect the letter with fatha with its matching letter with kasrah

Letter Section

Letter pronunciation and Writing

Activity 3 — Write the letters with kasrah

عِ عِ عِ عِ	ظِ ظِ	طِ طِ
قِ قِ	فِ فِ	غِ غِ غِ غِ
مِ مِ	لِ لِ	كِ كِ
وِ وِ	هِ هِ ﻬِ ﻫِ	نِ نِ
		يِ يِ يِ

27

Letter Section
Letter pronunciation and Writing

Activity 4 — Circle the letters with kasrah and write them in the box provided, then read the words

يَهِبْ	أَيِسَ	عَمِلَ	مَلِكَ
			لِ

فَهِمَ	عَوِجَ	أَمِنَ	تَرِنْ

Activity 5 — Read the words, then trace them

فَهِمَ	عَلِمَ	سَهِرَ
فهم	علم	سهر

عَوِجَ	شَهِدَ	تَرِنْ
عوج	شهد	ترن

28

Letter Section
Letter pronunciation and Writing

Activity 6 — Read the words, then trace them and separate them in to letters

فِ فِ	قِ قِ	كِ كِ
حَفِظَ	بَقِيَ	مَلِكِ
حفِظَ	بقِي	مَلِكِ
حَ + فِ + ظَ		

لِ لِ	مِ مِ	نِ نِ
عَلِمَ	عَمِلَ	تَرِنِ
عَلِمَ	عَمِلَ	تَرِنِ

هِ هِ هِ هِ	وِ	يِ يِ يِ
شَهِدَ	عَوِجَ	أَيِسَ
شَهِدَ	عَوِجَ	أَيِسَ

Quran Section
(Memorising the meaning of Quranic words)

لَيْلَةِ الْقَدْرِ

The night of Qadr
(in the month of Ramadan)

خَيْرٌ مِنْ

Better than

شَهْرٍ

Month

Homework

Activity 1 — Trace/write a kasrah where necessary

ع ‎ـع‎ ‎ـعـ‎	ظِ	ط
ق ‎قـ‎	ف ‎فـ‎	غ ‎غـ‎ ‎ـغـ‎ ‎ـغ‎
م ‎ـم‎	ل ‎لـ‎	ك ‎كـ‎
و	هـ ‎ـهـ‎ ‎ـه‎ ه	ن ‎نـ‎
		ي ‎ـي‎ ‎ـيـ‎

Homework

Activity 2 — Write the letters with kasrah

طِ طِ طِ	ظِ ظِ ظِ	عِ عِ عِ عِ عِ
غِ غِ غِ غِ غِ	فِ فِ فِ	قِ قِ قِ
كِ كِ كِ	لِ لِ لِ	مِ مِ مِ
نِ نِ نِ	هِ هِ هِ هِ هِ	وِ وِ وِ
يِ يِ يِ		

Lesson 3

Dammah

أُ بُ تُ ثُ

جُ حُ خُ دُ ذُ رُ زُ

سُ شُ صُ ضُ

Letter Section — Letter Recognition

Letter pronunciation and Writing

Listen and repeat the target letters with dammah after your teacher

ثُ ثُ	تُ تُ ۃُ ۃُ	بُ بُ	أُ ؤُ
دُ	خُ خُ	حُ حُ	جُ جُ
سُ سُ	زُ	رُ	ذُ
	ضُ ضُ	صُ صُ	شُ شُ

Letter Section
Letter pronunciation and Writing

Activity 1

Trace the letters with dammah

Letter Section
Letter pronunciation and Writing
Activity 3 — Write the letters with dammah

أُ ءُ اُ	بُ بُ	تُ تُ ةُ ةُ

ثُ ثُ	جُ جُ	حُ حُ

خُ خُ	دُ دُ	ذُ ذُ

رُ رُ	زُ زُ	سُ سُ

شُ شُ	صُ صُ	ضُ ضُ

Letter Section
Letter pronunciation and Writing

Activity 4 — Circle the letters with dammah and write them in the box provided, then read the words

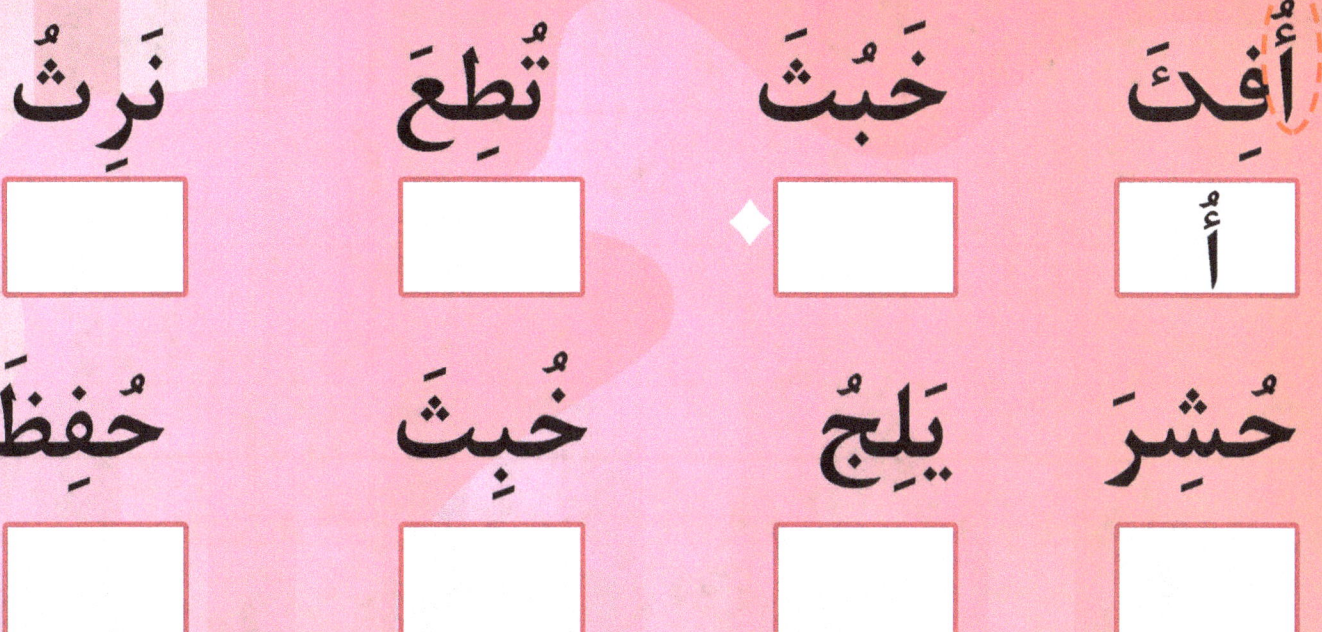

Activity 5 — Read the words, then trace them

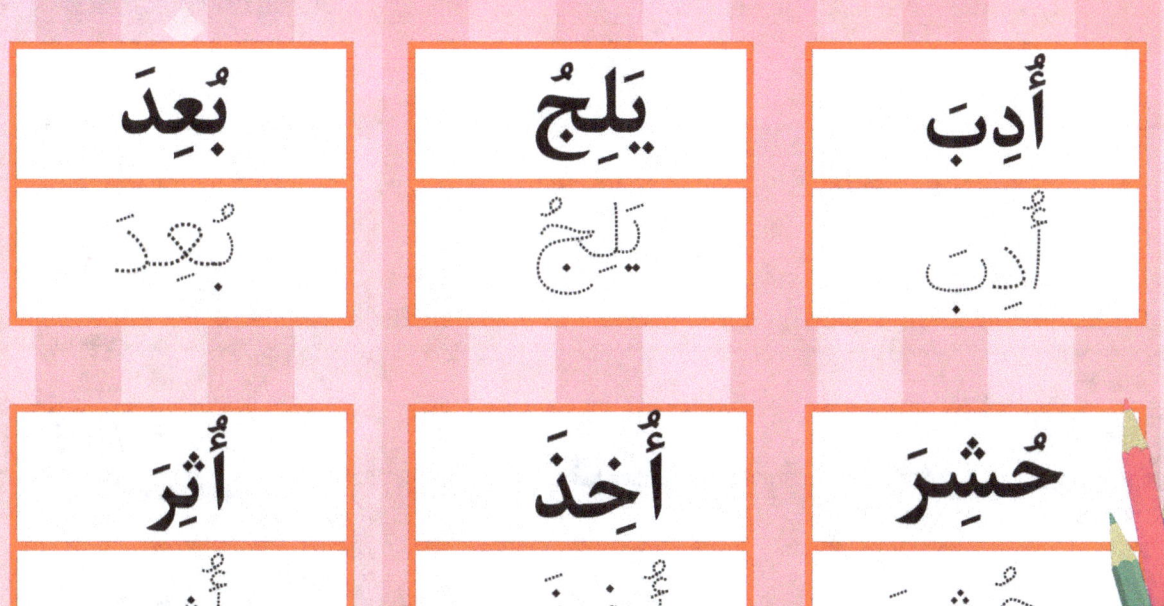

Letter Section
Letter pronunciation and Writing

Activity 6 — Read the words, then trace them and separate them in to letters

تُ ثَ ثُ ةَ ةُ	بُ بُ	أُ ءُ ءُ
تُطِعَ	بَعِيدَ	أَخِذَ
تُطِعَ	بَعِيدَ	أَخِذَ
		أُ + خِ + ذَ
حُ حُ	جُ جُ	ثُ ثُ
حُرِمَ	جُرِمَ	ثَبِتَ
حُرِمَ	جُرِمَ	ثَبِتَ
ذُ	دُ	خْ خُ
ذُبِلَ	دُعِيَ	خُمِسَ
ذُبِلَ	دُعِيَ	خُمِسَ

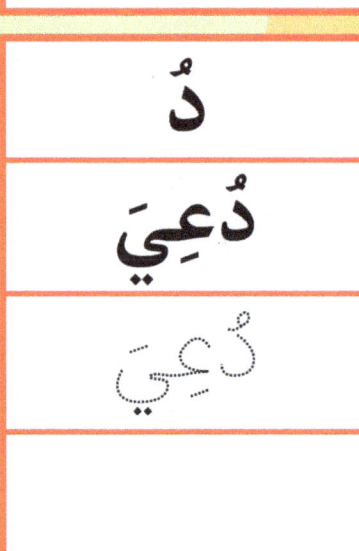

40

Quran Section
(Memorising the meaning of Quranic words)

الْمَلَائِكَةُ
The Angels

سَلَامٌ
Peace

Homework

Activity 1 — Trace/write a dammah where necessary

ثُ تُ ةُ ةُ	بُ بْ	أُ ئُ
حُ حْ	جُ جْ	ثُ ثْ
ذُ	د	خُ خْ
سُ سْ	ز	رُ
ش شْ	صُ صْ	ضُ ضْ

43

Homework

Activity 2 — Write the letters with dammah

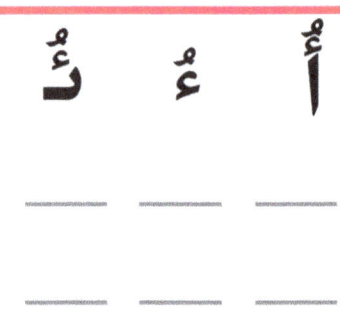

ثُ ثْ	جُ جْ	حُ حْ
أُ ءُ اُ	بُ بْ	تُ تْ ةُ ةْ

خُ خْ	دُ دْ	ذُ ذْ

رُ رْ	زُ زْ	سُ سْ

شُ شْ	صُ صْ	ضُ ضْ

Letter Section — Letter Recognition

Letter pronunciation and Writing

Listen and repeat the target letters with dammah after your teacher

Letter Section
Letter pronunciation and Writing

Activity 1
Trace the letters with dammah

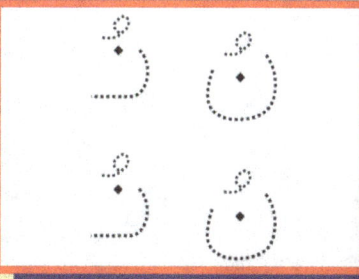

Letter Section

Letter pronunciation and Writing

Activity 3 — Write the letters with dammah

طُ طُ	ظُ ظُ	عُ عُ عُ عُ
فُ فُ	فُ فُ	غُ غُ غُ غُ
مُ مُ	لُ لُ	كُ كُ
وُ وُ	هُ هُ هُ هُ	نُ نُ
		يُ يُ يُ

49

Letter Section
Letter pronunciation and Writing

Activity 4 — Circle the letters with dammah and write them in the box provided, then read the words

لُعِبَ	لُعِنَ	كَمُلَ	نُفِخ
			نُ

هُوَ	يُرِدَ	هُجِرَ	وُعِدَ

Activity 5 — Read the words, then trace them

يَمُنَ	وُسِعَ	أُذُنُ
يَمُنَ	وُسِعَ	أُذُنُ

نُعِمَ	غَنَمٌ	هُدِمَ
نُعِمَ	غَنَمٌ	هُدِمَ

Letter Section
Letter pronunciation and Writing

Activity 6 — Read the words, then trace them and separate them in to letters

فُ فُ	قُ قُ	كُ كُ
فُقِدَ	خُلُقٌ	كُبِتَ
فُقِد	خُلُق	كُبِت
فُ + قِ + دَ		

لُ لُ	مُ مُ	نُ نُ
لُبِسَ	مُنِعَ	نُبِذَ
لُبِس	مُنِع	نُبِذ

هُ هُ هُ هُ	وُ	يُ يُ يُ
هُدِمَ	وُعِدَ	يُرِدِ
هُدِم	وُعِد	يُرِد

51

Quran Section
Memorising the Quranic moral sentence and its concept

رَّبِّ زِدْنِي عِلْمًا

(20:114)

O my Lord! Increase me in knowledge

Homework

Activity 1 — Trace/write a dammah where necessary

طُ	ظ	عُـ ـعُـ ـعُ عُ
غُـ ـغُـ ـغُ غُ	فُ فُ	قُ ق
كُ كـ	لُ لـ	مُ مـ
نـ ن	هُـ ـهُـ ـهُ هُ	وُ
		يـ ئـ ي

Homework

Activity 2 — Write the letters with dammah

طُ طُ	ظُ ظُ	عُ عُ عُ عُ
غُ غُ غُ غُ	فُ فُ	قُ قُ
كُ كُ	لُ لُ	مُ مُ
نُ نُ	هُ هُ هُ ةُ	وُ وُ
		يُ يُ يُ

Homework

Activity 3 — Colour the picture

رَّبِّ زِدْنِي عِلْمًا

(20:114)
O my Lord! Increase me in knowledge

Lesson 5

Fatha
Kasrah
Dammah

Letter Section — Letter Recognition

Letter pronunciation and Writing

Activity 1 — Read the letters with fatha, then write them

ثَ ثَ ثَ	تَ تَ ةَ	بَ بَ	أَ ءَ ئَ
دَ	خَ خَ	حَ حَ	جَ جَ
سَ سَ	زَ	رَ	ذَ
طَ	ضَ ضَ	صَ صَ	شَ شَ
فَ فَ	غَ غَ غَ غَ	عَ عَ عَ عَ	ظَ
مَ مَ	لَ لَ	كَ كَ	قَ قَ
يَ يَ يَ يَ	وَ	هَ هَ هَ ةَ	نَ نَ

Letter Section
Letter pronunciation and Writing

Activity 2 — Read the letters with kasra, then write them

ثِ ثِ ثِ	تِ تِ ةِ ةِ	بِ بِ	إِ ءِ ِ
دِ	خِ خِ	حِ حِ	جِ جِ
سِ سِ سِ	زِ	رِ	ذِ
طِ	ضِ ضِ	صِ صِ	شِ شِ
فِ فِ	غِ غِ غِ غِ	عِ عِ عِ عِ	ظِ
مِ مِ	لِ لِ	كِ كِ	قِ قِ
يِ يِ يِ	وِ	هِ هِ هِ هِ	نِ نِ

59

Letter Section
Letter pronunciation and Writing

Activity 3 — Read the letters with dammah, then write them

ثُ ثُ ثُ	تُ ثُ ةُ ةُ	بُ بُ	أُ ءُ
دُ	خُ خُ	حُ حُ	جُ جُ
سُ سُ	زُ	رُ	ذُ
طُ	ضُ ضُ	صُ صُ	شُ شُ
فُ فُ	غُ غُ غُ غُ	عُ عُ عُ	ظُ
مُ مُ	لُ لُ	كُ كُ	قُ قُ
يُ يُ يُ	وُ	هُ هُ هُ ةُ	نُ نُ

60

Letter Section
Letter pronunciation and Writing

Activity 4 — Circle the letters with fatha, then read the words

مُنِعَ	أُمِرَ	فَزِعَ	قُبِلَ
سَلِمَ	إِبِلَ	مَطَرٌ	جَمَلٌ

Circle the letters with kasra, then read the words

حَسُنَ	شُرِبَ	جُعِلَ	فُصِلَ
أُكِلَ	قُسِمَ	قُبِلَ	فُزِعَ

Circle the letters with dammah, then read the words

جَبَلٌ	صَغُرَ	قَمَرٌ	كُتِبُ
يَعِدُ	مَطَرٌ	يَلِجُ	ضُرِبَ

Letter Section
Letter pronunciation and Writing

Activity 5 — Read the words, then separate them in to letters

غَنَمٌ	كُتِبَ	جَعَلَ
		جَ + عَ + لَ

مَطَرٌ	جَلَسَ	رَضِيَ

Activity 6 — Read the words, then trace them

صَغُرَ	حَسُنَ	نَعَمَ	يَلِجُ
صَغُرَ	حَسُنَ	نَعَمَ	يَلِجُ

قَبَضَ	سَلِمَ	قَمَرٌ	مُنِعَ
قَبَضَ	سَلِمَ	قَمَرٌ	مُنِعَ

Quran Section
(Memorising the Surah and understanding the concept)

بِسْمِ اللَّهِ الرَّحْمَنِ الرَّحِيمِ

أَلَمْ تَرَ كَيْفَ فَعَلَ رَبُّكَ بِأَصْحَابِ الْفِيلِ (1)

أَلَمْ يَجْعَلْ كَيْدَهُمْ فِي تَضْلِيلٍ (2)

وَأَرْسَلَ عَلَيْهِمْ طَيْرًا أَبَابِيلَ (3)

تَرْمِيهِمْ بِحِجَارَةٍ مِنْ سِجِّيلٍ (4) فَجَعَلَهُمْ كَعَصْفٍ مَأْكُولٍ (5)

Surah Al-Fil

Surah Al-Fil tells a story about an event that happened the year Prophet Mohammad (S.A.A) was born. Its about a man named Abrahah, the king of Yemen who heard about the fame of Mecca and the Ka'bah. He got jealous and greedy so he decided to create a very large army and get some elephants to attack Mecca and destroy the Ka'bah, but when the elephants got close to the Ka'bah they stopped moving and wouldn't attack. Allah sent birds carrying stones, when the birds reached the army they dropped the stones and killed the army.

Homework

Activity 1 — Colour the letters in their assigned colour

Letters with fatha red | Letters with kasra blue | Letters with dammah green

ثَ ثَ	ثُ ثُ ةُ ةُ	بِ بِ	أَ ءَ ئَ
دِ	خَ خَ	حَ حِ	جُ جُ
سَ سَ	زِ	رُ	ذَ
طُ	ضَ ضَ	صِ صِ	شُ شُ
فِ فِ	غَ غُ غُ غُ	عَ عَ عَ عَ	ظِ
مُ مُ	لَ لَ	كِ كِ	قُ قُ
يَ يَ يَ	وِ	هُ هُ هُ ةُ	نَ نَ

Homework

Activity 2 — Read the words, then write them

سَمِعَ	هَرَبَ	جَزَعَ
....	....	....
كَرُمَ	نَبَتَ	كُتِبَ
....	....	....
مَطَرٌ	مُنِعَ	صَغُرَ
....	....	....
رُسُلَ	قَمَرٌ	غَنَمٌ
....	....	....

Lesson 6

Fatha
Kasrah
Dammah

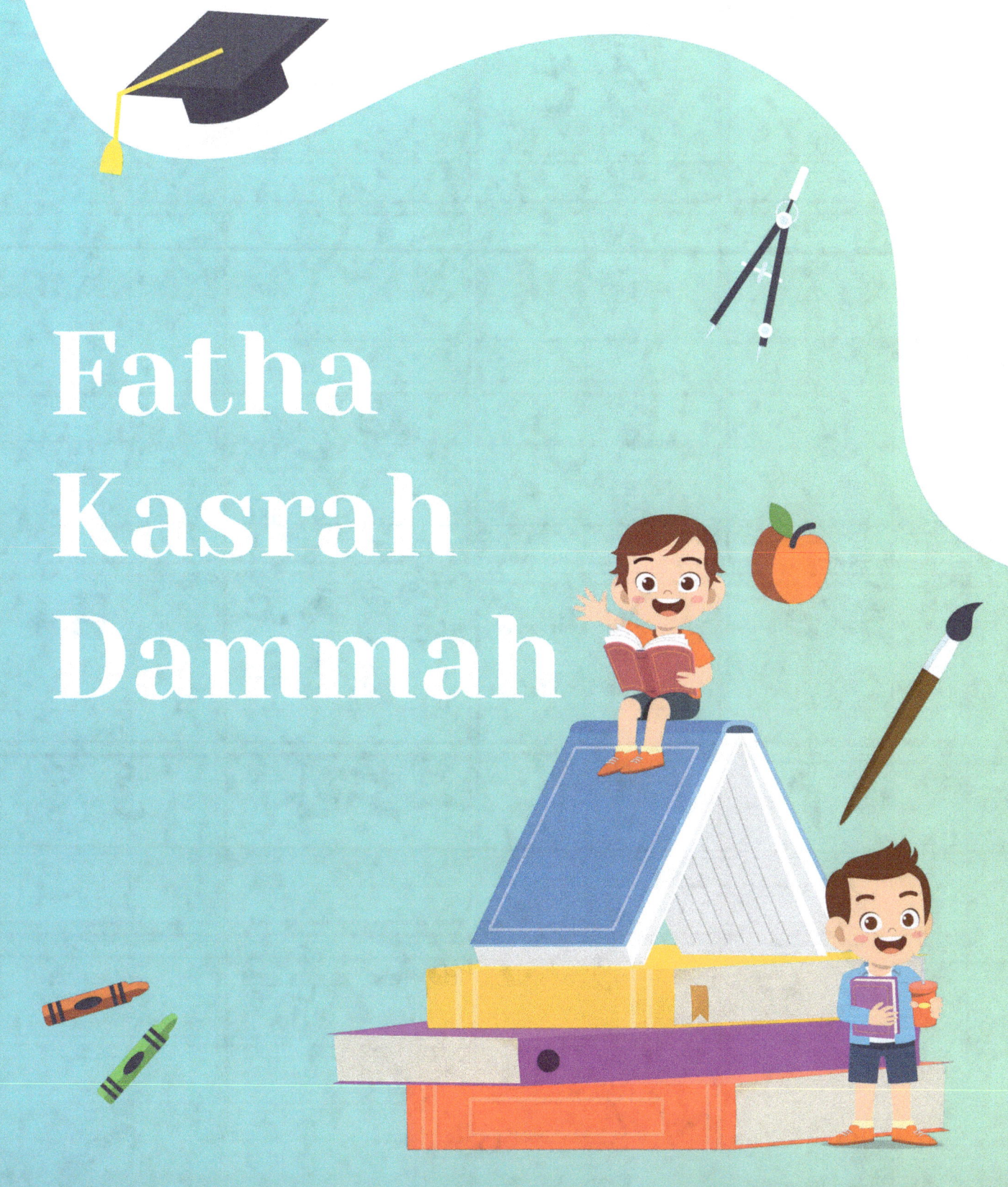

Letter Section — Letter Recognition

Letter pronunciation and Writing

Activity 1 — Read the letters with fatha, then write them

ثَ ثَ ثَ	تَ تَ تَ ةَ	بَ بَ	أَ ءَ ئَ
دَ	خَ خَ	حَ حَ	جَ جَ
سَ سَ	زَ	رَ	ذَ
طَ	ضَ ضَ	صَ صَ	شَ شَ
فَ فَ	غَ غَ غَ غَ	عَ عَ عَ عَ	ظَ
مَ مَ	لَ لَ	كَ كَ	قَ قَ
يَ يَ يَ يَ	وَ	هَ هَ هَ ةَ	نَ نَ

Letter Section
Letter pronunciation and Writing

Activity 2 — Read the letters with Kasrah, then write them

ثِ ثِ ثِ	تِ تِـ ةِ ةِ	بِ بِـ	إِ ءِ بِ
دِ	خِ خِـ	حِ حِـ	جِ جِـ
سِ سِـ	زِ	رِ	ذِ
طِ	ضِ ضِـ	صِ صِـ	شِ شِـ
فِ فِـ	غِ غِـ غِـ غِ	عِ عِـ عِـ عِ	ظِ
مِ مِـ	لِ لِـ	كِ كِـ	قِ قِـ
يِ يِـ يِـ	وِ	هِ هِـ هِـ ةِ	نِ نِـ

69

Letter Section
Letter pronunciation and Writing

Activity 3 — Read the letters with Dammah, then write them

ثُ ثُ ثُ	ثُ ثُ ةُ ةُ	بُ بُ	أُ ءُ
دُ	خُ خُ	حُ حُ	جُ جُ
سُ سُ	زُ	رُ	ذُ
طُ	ضُ ضُ	صُ صُ	شُ شُ
فُ فُ	غُ غُ غُ غُ	عُ عُ عُ عُ	ظُ
مُ مُ	لُ لُ	كُ كُ	قُ قُ
يُ يُ يُ يُ	وُ	هُ هُ هُ ةُ	نُ نُ

70

Letter Section
Letter pronunciation and Writing

Activity 4 Circle the letters with Fatha, then read the words

كَتِبَ   مُنِعَ   قُسِمَ   شُرِبَ

فُزِعَ   يَلِجُ   ثُبِتَ   فُتِحَ

Circle the letters with kasrah, then read the words

سَلِمَ   أَمِرَ   أُكِلَ   يَعِدُ

رَضِىَ   قُبِلَ   نُفِخَ   خُلِقَ

Circle the letters with dammah, then read the words

جُعِلَ   حُشِرَ   دُرِجَ   حُبِطَ

رُدِفَ   أُذِنَ   ذُبِحَ   زُعِمَ

71

Letter Section
Letter pronunciation and Writing

Activity 5 — Read the words, then separate them into letters

دُعِيَ	مُنِعَ	كَرُمَ
دُ + عِ + يَ		

سَمِعَ	قَمَرُ	غَنَمُ

Activity 6 — Read the words, then trace them

كَرُمَ	مَطَرُ	حَسُنَ
كرم	مطر	حسن

جَمَلُ	قُسِمَ	جَلَسَ
جمل	قسم	جلس

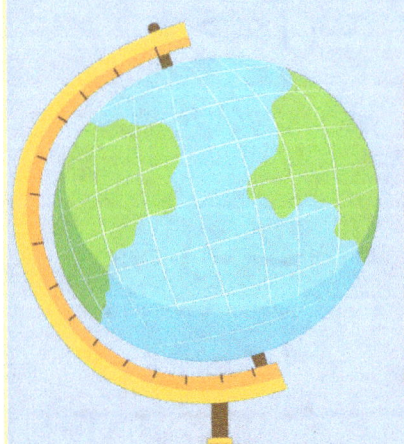

Quran Section
(Memorising the meaning of Quranic words)

الْفِيلِ

The elephant

 كَيْدَ

Evil plan

Homework

Activity 1 — Colour the letters in their assigned colour

Letters with fatha red | Letters with kasra blue | Letters with dammah green

بَ	إِ	سِ	شُ
ذَ	دِ	زُ	رَ
لِ	كَ	قَ	فِ
أَ	بَ	ثِ	تُ
صُ	خِ	حُ	جَ
عَ	ظُ	طِ	ضَ
هَـ	نِ	مَ	غِ

Homework

Activity 2 — Read the words, then write them

وَعَدَ	هُدِمَ	كُبِتَ

مُنِعَ	لُبِسَ	ذُهِبَ

نُبِذَ	كُتِبَ	فُقِدَ

نُفِخَ	نُعِمَ	غَنَمُ

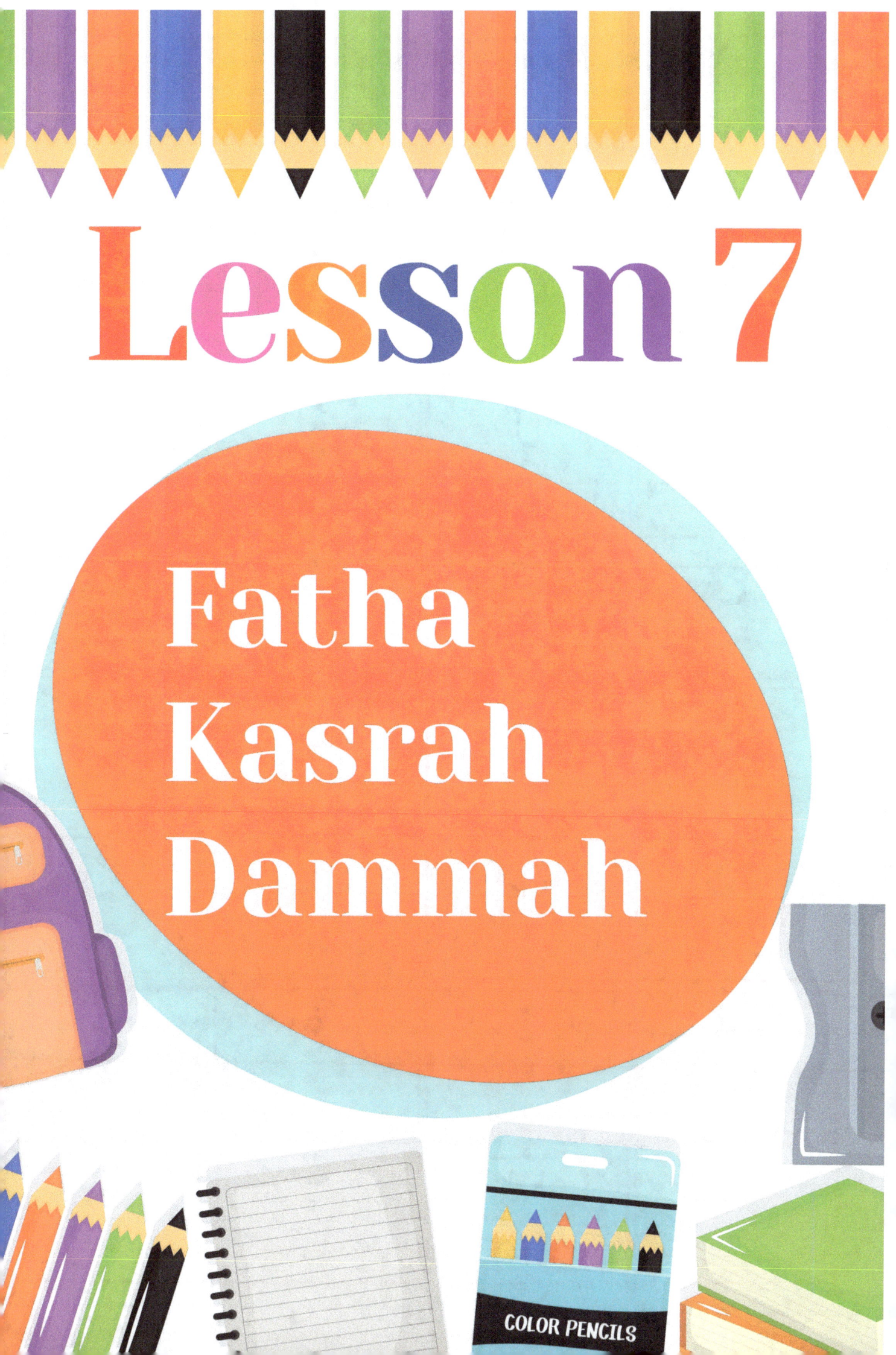

Letter Section — Letter Recognition

Activity 1 Colour the letters in their assigned colour

Letters with fatha red | Letters with kasra blue | Letters with dammah green

رِ	يَ	وَ	هُ
مَ	لِ	كُ	زَ
خَ	جَ	قِ	فُ
دُ	ذَ	شِ	سُ
ضَ	صِ	طُ	نَ
هِ	حِ	غَ	عُ
أُ	بُ	تِ	ثَ

Letter Section
Letter pronunciation and Writing

Activity 2 — Read the words, then write them

فَرِحَ	بُعِثَ	كَثُرَ	أَذِنَ
....	....	....	....

عُبِدَ	قَعَدَ	شَرَحَ	رَكِبَ
....	....	....	....

قُرِءَ	كَمُلَ	وُعِدَ	نُفِخَ
....	....	....	....

Letter Section
Letter pronunciation and Writing

Activity 3 — Draw the assigned shapes around each letter

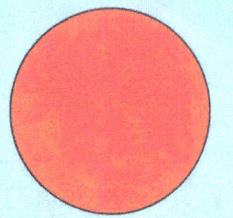
Letters in Fatha

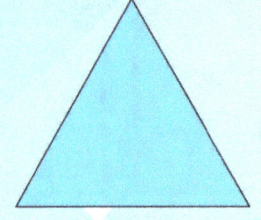
Letters in Kasrah

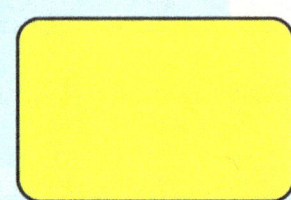
Letters in Dammah

قِ	كُ	زَ	رِ	هُ	شِ	سَ
لِ	وِ	يُ	نَ	دَ	زُ	فِ
هَ	بَ	تَ	رِ	دُ	مُ	ذُ
		عَ	جِ	حُ	أَ	

Letter Section
Letter pronunciation and Writing

Activity 4 — Read the words, then separate them into letters

أَذِنَ	أُمِرَ	رُسُلِ
أَ + ذِ + نَ	....	....

رَضِيَ	وُعِدَ	رُوِيَ
....	....	....

خَشِيَ	جُعِلَ	خُلِقَ
....	....	....

سَمِعَ	وُضِعَ	سَمِعَ
....	....	....

Quran Section
(Memorising the meaning of Quranic words)

طَيْرًا

Bird

حِجَارَةٌ

Stone

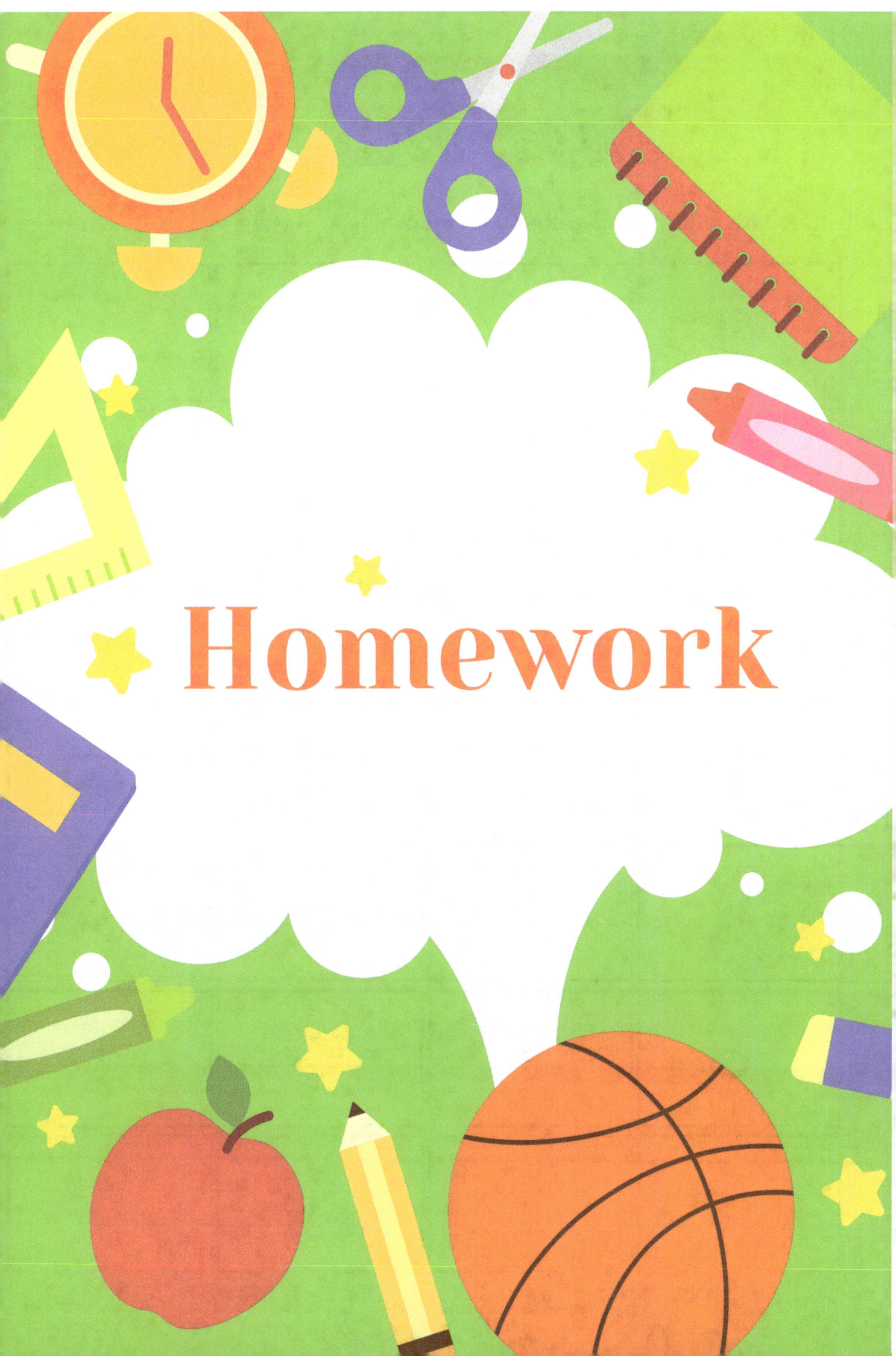

Homework

Activity 1 — Colour the letters in their assigned colour

Letters with fatha red   Letters with kasra blue   Letters with dammah green

كَ	سُ	زِ	رَ
مُ	لِ	غُ	عِ
ذِ	دُ	قَ	فِ
صَ	طِ	هُـ	يَ
جَ	صُ	خِ	ضُ
ثُ	مَ	بُ	إِ
وَ	شِ	أَ	ثُ

Homework

Activity 2 — Read the words, then write them

مُنِعَ	جُعِلَ	كُتِبَ
....	....	....

صَغُرَ	نَبَتَ	كَرُمَ
....	....	....

هَرَبَ	وُعِدَ	غَنُمَ
....	....	....

وُعِظَ	رَضِيَ	وَرَدَ
....	....	....

Letter Section — Letter Recognition

Activity 1 Colour the letters in their assigned colour

Letters with fatha red | Letters with kasra blue | Letters with dammah green

إِ	زَ	رُ	هِ
ظَ	طِ	شِ	سُ
سِ	نَ	لِ	كُ
فِ	ثُ	تِ	بَ
ثَ	جُ	رِ	قَ
أَ	ضُ	صِ	خَ

Letter Section
Letter pronunciation and Writing

Activity 2 — Read the words, then write them

فُتِحَ	خَسَفَ	جُمِعَ	خَلَقَ
كُبِتَ	رُسُلَ	بَصَرُ	نُفِخَ
ذَكَرَ	عَلِمَ	رَضِيَ	جَعَلَ

88

Letter Section
Letter pronunciation and Writing

Activity 3 Draw the assigned shapes around each letter

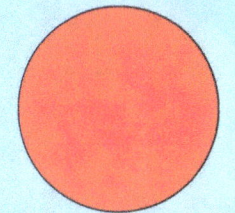
Letters in Fatha

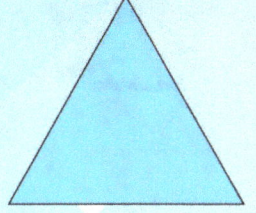
Letters in Kasrah

Letters in Dammah

طَ	وُ	زِ	رَ	هُـ	شَ سِ
دِ	مَ	فُ	ظِ	ضَ	صِ
كَ	هَ	نِ	سُ	أُ	قِ ذُ
		يِ	جُ	مَ	خِ

89

Letter Section
Letter pronunciation and Writing

Activity 4 — Read the words, then separate them into letters

دُعِيَ	حُشِرَ	عُثِرَ
دُ + عِ + يَ	....	....

أُخِذَ	يَلِجُ	حُفِظَ
....	....	....

عَمِلَ	بَقِيَ	شَهِدَ
....	....	....

رَدِفَ	شَجَرَةِ	رَحِمَ
....	....	....

90

Quran Section
Memorising the Quranic moral sentence and its concept

فَأَصْلِحُوا بَيْنَ أَخَوَيْكُمْ
(49:10)

So make peace among your brothers

Homework

Activity 1 — Colour the letters in their assigned colour

Letters with fatha red   Letters with kasra blue   Letters with dammah green

لَ	كُ	قِ	فُ
حَ	شَ	سِ	جُ
طِ	زِ	تِ	بُ
ظَ	رَ	خُ	حِ
غَ	نَ	ضُ	صِ
إِ	وَ	زُ	مِ

Homework

Activity 2 — Read the words, then write them

طُبِعَ	هُبِطَ	ذُبِحَ
....	....	....

خَسِرَ	تَصِفُ	أَذِنَ
....	....	....

ذُهِبَ	بَخِلَ	رَبِحَ
....	....	....

وُجِدَ	شُكَرَ	وُضِعَ
....	....	....

Lesson 9

Revision

Letter Section — Letter Recognition
Letter pronunciation and Writing

Activity 1 — Read the letters with fatha, then write them

ثَ ثَ ثَ	تَ تَ ةَ ةَ	بَ بَ	أَ ءَ ئَ
دَ	خَ خَ	حَ حَ	جَ جَ
سَ سَ	زَ	رَ	ذَ
طَ	ضَ ضَ	صَ صَ	شَ شَ
فَ فَ فَ	غَ غَ غَ غَ	عَ عَ عَ عَ	ظَ
مَ مَ	لَ لَ	كَ كَ	قَ قَ
يَ يَ يَ يَ	وَ	هَ هَ هَ ةَ	نَ نَ

Letter Section
Letter pronunciation and Writing

Activity 2 — Read the letters with Kasrah, then write them

ثِ ثٍ	تِ تِ ةِ ةٍ	بِ بٍ	إِ ءِ

دِ	خِ خٍ	حِ حٍ	جِ جٍ

سِ سٍ	زِ	رِ	ذِ

طِ	ضِ ضٍ	صِ صٍ	شِ شٍ

فِ فٍ	غِ غٍ غٍ غٍ	عِ عِ عِ عٍ	ظِ

مِ مٍ	لِ لٍ	كِ كٍ	قِ قٍ

يِ يٍ يٍ	وِ	هِ هِ هِ هٍ	نِ نٍ

Letter Section
Letter pronunciation and Writing

Activity 3 — Read the letters with Dammah, then write them

ثُ ثُ ثُ	ثُ ثَةُ ثُةُ	بُ بُ	أُ ءُ
دُ	خُ خُ	حُ حُ	جُ جُ
سُ سُ	زُ	رُ	ذُ
طُ	ضُ ضُ	صُ صُ	شُ شُ
فُ فُ	غُ غُ غُ غُ	عُ عُ عُ عُ	ظُ
مُ مُ	لُ لُ	كُ كُ	قُ قُ
يُ يُ يُ يُ	وُ	هُ هُ هُ ةُ	نُ نُ

Letter Section
Letter Pronunciation and Writing

Activity 4 — Count the letters with Fatha, Kasrah, Dammah in the Quranic sentences, then write the number of each in the boxes below

	فَمَآ أَوْجَفْتُمْ عَلَيْهِ
	سورة الحَشْر (6)

Fatha َ	Kasrah ِ	Dammah ُ

	قَالَ تَزْرَعُونَ سَبْعَ سِنِينَ
	سورة يُوسُف (47)

Fatha َ	Kasrah ِ	Dammah ُ

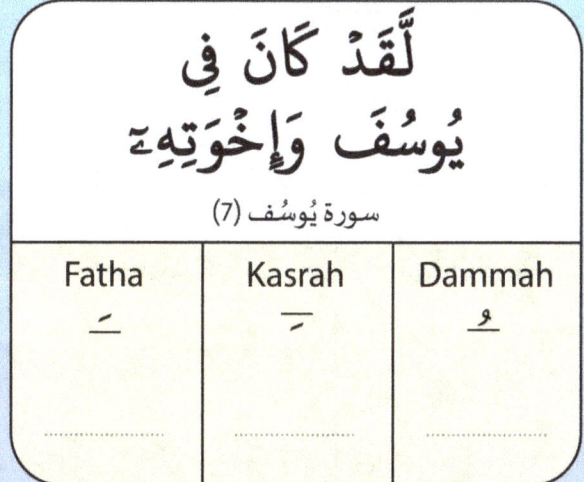

لَقَدْ كَانَ فِي يُوسُفَ وَإِخْوَتِهِ

سورة يُوسُف (7)

Fatha َ	Kasrah ِ	Dammah ُ

	إِن يَشَأْ يُذْهِبْكُمْ
	سورة النِّسَاء (133)

Fatha َ	Kasrah ِ	Dammah ُ

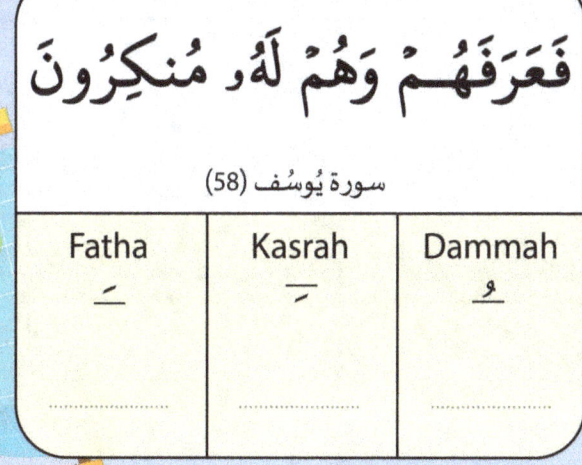

فَعَرَفَهُمْ وَهُمْ لَهُ مُنكِرُونَ

سورة يُوسُف (58)

Fatha َ	Kasrah ِ	Dammah ُ

	وَلَا يَجِدُونَ فِي صُدُورِهِمْ
	سورة الحَشْر (9)

Fatha َ	Kasrah ِ	Dammah ُ

Letter Section
Letter pronunciation and Writing
Activity 2 — Read the words, then trace them

تَصِفُ	بَقِيَ	نُزِلَ	خَطِفَ
ذَهَبَ	خَسِرَ	عُثِرَ	أَثِرَ
طُبِعَ	كُبِتَ	أَذِنَ	شِيَةَ
خَبُثَ	ذُبِحَ	هُبِطَ	مَلِكِ

Quran Section
Quranic Game

Separate the class into 3-4 groups. The teacher picks a word from a previously memorised Surah and writes down a space for each letter in the word. Each group takes turns guessing a letter. If the group is right the teacher writes the letter down and awards the group 5 points. If they are wrong the group gets no points and it the next group's turn. When the letters are all revealed the team with the most points wins.

Homework

Activity 1 Read the words, then separate them into letters

عَمِلَ	خُلِقَ	شَهِدَ	ذَهَبَ
			ذَ + هَـ + بَ

وُضِعَ	نُبِذَ	جُعِلَ	عَجِبَ

عَلِمَ	ظُلِمَ	حَضَرَ	وُعِظَ

وُلِدَ	سَمِعَ	شَجَرَةٌ	قُضِيَ

103

Homework

Activity 2 Read the words, then write them

نَسِيَ	خَشِعَ	كُتِبَ	قُرِءَ
يَئِسَ	رَكِبَ	غَرِقَ	حُفِرَ
أَذِنَ	كَثُرَ	بُعِثَ	قَعَدَ
فَرِحَ	ظُلِمَ	عُبِدَ	شَرَحَ

104

www.ingramcontent.com/pod-product-compliance
Lightning Source LLC
Chambersburg PA
CBHW080857010526
44107CB00058B/2602